COTSW
RAMBLES

25 short walks in the finest
part of the Cotswolds

Harry Hargreaves

Published by
Thornhill Press
24 Moorend Road
Cheltenham

THORNHILL PRESS

© Harry Hargreaves

ISBN 0 946328 196

3rd Edition 1988

The maps are based upon the relevant Ordnance Survey
maps with the permission of the Controller of
Her Majesty's Stationery Office, Crown Copyright reserved.

Printed by Logos Ltd.

AUTHOR'S NOTE

As a result of an earlier book of Cotswold Rambles produced in collaboration with Peter Drinkwater, many people have said that a collection of shorter walks would be welcome, and have suggested that I should compile one. This book therefore has been produced to meet this need. This is the third edition of this book and a few corrections have been made.

I am appreciative of all the people and the organisations who by their activities in keeping open and conserving the countryside, have helped to make possible the production of this book. Special mention must be made of the Cotswold Wardens, The Ramblers' Association, The Common Open Spaces and Footpaths Preservation Society, The National Trust and The Countryside Commission. My special thanks are due to the Footpaths Section of the Gloucestershire County Council for placing at my disposal a room in which I could examine unhurriedly large scale maps and for producing photstat copies of maps. The latter obviated the need for frequent visits to Gloucester yet enabled me to learn the exact position of footpaths. The Gloucestershire County Council have also been most helpful in communicating with landowners in order to have obstructions removed.

I would like to thank all those ramblers and especially the members of the Evesham Rambling Club who have walked with me during the preparation of this book and added to my enjoyment.

My thanks also to Peter Price for producing the excellent map on the back of this book.

Finally all those who have been interested in the preparation of this book are very appreciative of those farmers who have been helpful in removing obstructions and have co-operated in the clearance of footpaths.

HARRY HARGREAVES

THE COUNTRY CODE

Please remember as you walk throughout the countryside to respect the privacy and livelihood of those who live in the country. The Country Code asks you to:-

1. Guard against all risk of fire.
2. Fasten all gates.
3. Keep dogs under proper control.
4. Keep to paths across farmland.
5. Avoid damaging fences, hedges and walls.
6. Leave no litter.
7. Safeguard water supplies.
8. Protect wild life, plants and trees.
9. Go carefully on country roads.
10. Respect the life of the countryside.

Ramble 9, near Shenberrow.

INTRODUCTION

This book contains rambles most of which could be completed in a morning or an afternoon or an evening. The shortest walk is three miles only, several are between four and six miles, and there is one of nine miles. The walks require care and concentration.

The rambles are in the part of the Cotswolds between Broadway in the north and Cirencester in the south, an area considered by many who love the Cotswolds to be the most beautiful. Bredon is not strictly in the Cotswolds but it is so near and so lovely that the stretch had to be made.

It is hoped that the narrative of each ramble is so detailed that it is not necessary to use a map. However the map at the beginning of each ramble is a copy of the Ordnance Map on the 1/50000 scale (approximately 1¼″ to the mile). This will enable the rambler to see the ramble in outline and if the narrative is departed from it should help to get back to the correct way.

The Ordnance Map for the area on the 1/50000 scale is stated at the beginning of each ramble.

It is stating the obvious to say: Make sure you get to the right starting point. At the beginning of each ramble a place is named which is on the map on the back of the book. From this named place a description is given of how to get to the starting point.

Each ramble starts and finishes at the same place.

Allow not less than one hour for each two miles of rambling.

Whilst the Cotswolds do not have the dangers of mountains or wild moorlands some precautions will ensure that enjoyment is not marred. Therefore make sure your clothing and especially your footwear are comfortable and adequate and see that you have sufficient time to complete a ramble before sunset.

While an endeavour has been made to ensure that each ramble follows throughout its length existing 'Rights of Way' and every possible care has been taken to ensure the accuracy of all information in the book, the Author and Publishers cannot accept any liability for the accuracy of the information given or for its interpretation by readers.

Ramble 8, near Cutsdean Village.

Ramble 9, going down to Snowshill.

INDEX

Ramble 12, Stanton.

Ramble 11, the Hinchwick Valley.

GUITING POWER, NAUNTON, BARTON
Distance 6 miles.
Map OS 163 in the 1:50,000 series.
Starting point: Grid reference 095248. Guiting Power.

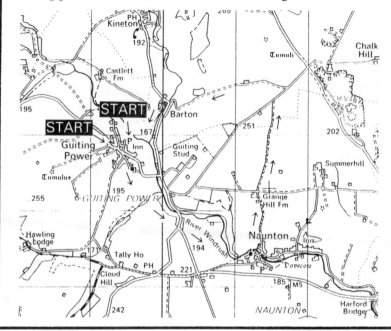

Guiting was apparently the old name of the upper River Windrush and means "torrent". The Guiting Power church, although it has been considerably reconstructed, is still interesting; the north entrance is Norman and has a beautiful arch.

From the centre of the village, go up the lane to the church. Just before the church go through the iron gate. Go ahead over the wooden fence. Follow the path through the field to a gate on the left. Do not go through the gate but follow a wall which is on the left, to a facing wall. Cross a stile. Take an indefinite path bearing left passing within 30 yards of an isolated oak tree to the left of the path. Descend to a stone bridge over a stream and go past a nature reserve which is on the right. Proceed ahead up the incline to a kissing gate. Continue in the same direction over the next two fields, along a ridge track to the road.

Cross the road and go up the lane opposite. After 300 yards go through a gate on the left, at the beginning of a small roadside wood, and then turn right to follow the headland with trees on the right. At the end of the trees go through another gate and continue in the same direction along a bank. At the end of the bank pass into the next field with a hedge and trees on the right. Follow alongside these past a gate to a stile on the right in the corner of the field. Go over the stile to the road and turn left. Pass the church, cross the river and turn right into Naunton. (Refreshment available at the Black Horse Inn). 2 miles have now been walked.

From the Black Horse Inn walk back along the road used on entering the village. Instead of turning towards the church to cross the river, go straight on up the rising road. Continue up this road for ½ mile to Grange Hill Farm. Cross the minor road and proceed for ¾ mile along a cart track to another minor road. Turn right and in 250 yards take the cart track on the left. Follow this over four fields and go over a fence into a narrow passage which descends to the left into Barton. Turn right and cross the River Windrush by a road bridge. The house on the right has a magnificent bank of snowdrops in February.

Take the first turn on the left with some buildings on the right and a pond on the left. Continue past a farm road on the right which leads to Castlett Farm. Go ahead between the farm buildings and pass over three stiles. Then bear right along a path and make for the left corner of a facing hedge running to the right. Continue in the same direction with a hedge on the right. Cross a stone stile in this hedge and turn left to go downhill. Cross a tributary of the River Windrush by a wooden bridge and ascend to a stile. Cross this into a lane and follow it upwards into Guiting Power. (4 miles have been walked from Naunton making a 6 mile walk.)

GUITING POWER, CASTLETT STUD, NEAR KINETON, GUITING WOOD

A walk which combines charming woodland with open views.
Distance 6 miles or alternatively 4½ miles.
Map OS 163 in the 1:50,000 series.
Starting point: Grid reference 095248. The village of
Guiting Power.

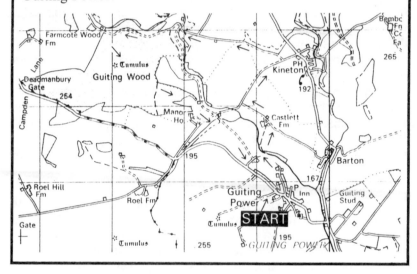

From the Farmers Arms Inn walk towards the village green.

Go past the post office and then take the first road on the right.
Walk along this for about 500 yards to a gate. Go through this and
continue down the grass track. At the bottom of the descent turn
right and cross a stream by a stone bridge. There is evidence of a
mill stream here and there is a brick storage in the bank. Ascend to
a gate. Continue between fence to Castlett Farm seen in front. Go
through the farm and then continue ahead with a cottage on the
right along the farm drive to the road.

Turn right. In a little over ½ a mile where the village of Kineton
can be seen in the distance, turn left along a rough farm track, and
in ¾ mile at a cross track, continue ahead to the road in Guiting
Wood near the pumping station.

At this point the decision must be made whether to do the 4½
mile walk or the 6 mile walk.

11

First a description of the 4½ mile walk.

At the road, turn left and walk for about ¾ mile to a cottage on the right. This is Pump Bottom. The longer walk of 6 miles rejoins at this point.

So now the description of the longer walk.

Instead of turning left at the road where the alternative description began, go straight ahead.

In about ¾ mile where the road turns to the right, there are 2 signposted tracks into the wood on the left. Take the left hand one i.e. the one straight ahead which ascends through the wood. This wood is the property of the Corpus Christi College, Oxford but there is a right of way. Continue along the track without any deviation to where the wood on the left finishes and the track turns right through a gate.

Do not turn right but go straight ahead down an overgrown path with an open field on the left and a wood on the right. Follow the track to a stile and continue to the right of a cottage to the road at Pump Bottom. Turn right.

This is the point which connects with the alternative shorter walk.

In 300 yards cross over the road into a cart way. In a short distance Castlett Farm will be seen on the left on the other side of the valley. In ½ mile, at a farm road which runs uphill to the right, turn left and immediately on the left take a green path down through a thicket to a stream. Continue ahead, with the stream on the left, to ascend to a road which leads into Guiting Power. Turn left to the village green.

PINNOCK WARREN, NEWTOWN, ROEL FARM, PUMP BOTTOM, GUITING WOOD

A fine short ramble, mostly woodland and a charming unspoilt valley.
Distance 4½ miles.
Map OS 163 in the 1:50,000 series.
Starting point: Grid reference 069270.

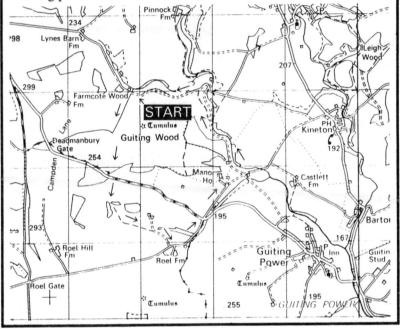

To get to the starting point from Winchcombe; coming into Winchcombe on the A.46 from the north with the George Hotel on the left, go down the first road on the left past the hotel. This road passes the main entrance to Sudeley Castle which is on the right. In about ¾ mile past this entrance the drive to Sudeley Lodge will be seen on the right, but continue ahead up the hill. Take the first turn left S.P. Ford Cutsdean. In 1¼ miles take the right hand road at a fork. (Do not be put off by the sign "Unsuitable for cars". It is only unsuitable because it is difficult for two cars to pass each other.) In ¾ mile there is an attractive cottage on the left with a stream in front. This is Pinnock Warren. Park a car a little distance past this cottage.

This is the start of the walk.

In about 200 yards past the cottages, at a left hand bend of the road, there are two waymarked paths on the right going into the wood. Take the one going to the right. In about 600 yards continue ahead over some waymarked tracks. In wet weather mud can make this very difficult. Continue ahead along the definite track to a T junction with another track. Turn right and go ahead to the road.

Turn left and go through the first gate on the right. Continue ahead keeping a fence and hedge on the right, to the gate straight ahead between two woods. Go through this gate and skirt the edge of the wood on the left to a gate. Pass through this gate, bear left and continue to a farm road which leaves some cottages on the left. This is Newtown. Go through the gate at the end of this farm road and cross the valley to a rising diagonal cart track on the opposite side and to the left. Continue to the road at Roel Farm. Turn left and go over the next cross roads.

In a further ½ mile (ignore two tracks on the left which go towards a distinguished house) at a point where there is a road on the left and a cartway on the right, turn down the road on the left. Follow this without deviation for 1¾ miles through the Guiting Wood to the beginning of the walk.

DEADMANBURY GATE, GUITING WOOD, NEWTOWN, ROEL FARM, CAMPDEN LANE

An easy pleasant walk with woodland and ancient tracks.
Distance 4 miles.
Map OS 163 in the 1:50,000 series.
Starting point: Grid reference 057263.
2½ miles S.E. of Winchcombe.

The starting point will probably be approached from Winchcombe.

In this case proceed from the George Hotel in the direction of the church and take the first turn on the left which goes to Sudeley Castle. Go along this road for 1¼ miles to the top of the hill and a little beyond at the fork, bear left (signposted Guiting Power). In a further ¼ mile the entrance to Farmcote Wood Farm will be passed on the left. Continue for a further 400 yards to a rough parking place on the left where there is a bridleway sign.

This is Deadmanbury Gate and is the start of the walk. The County Archivist is not able to establish any facts as to the derivation of the name.

Do *not* go along the signposted bridleway but descend on a track

15

to the right of it to a path going to the right. Go along this path to the right so as to have a hedge and open field on the left and the wood on the right. In just over ½ mile a signposted crossing of tracks is reached. Turn right along a definite track. In wet weather mud may make this track very difficult. Ascend to a T junction of tracks; turn right and go to the road.

At the road turn left and go through the first gate on the right. Continue ahead keeping fence and hedge on the right to the gate straight ahead between two woods. Go through this gate and skirt the edge of the wood on the left to another gate: passing through this gate, bear left and continue to a farm road. Pass through a gateway which leaves some cottages on the left. This is Newtown.

At the end of this farm road go through a gate, cross the valley in front and bear left to ascend to a cart track. This leads to a gate. Go through this to the road at Roel Farm. Turn right and in 1 mile turn right down Campden Lane, a farm road, to go past Roel Hill Farm. In 1 mile, from the beginning of the farm road, a road is reached. Turn left and in 100 yards the beginning and end of the walk is reached.

NAUNTON, GRANGE HILL FARM, EYFORD PARK

From the pleasant village of Naunton pass along a beautiful section of the Windrush followed by Parkland.
Distance 7 miles.
Map OS 163 in the 1:50,000 series.
Starting point: Grid reference 120235, the village of Naunton.
Naunton is off the Andoversford to Stow-on-the-Wold section of B4068.

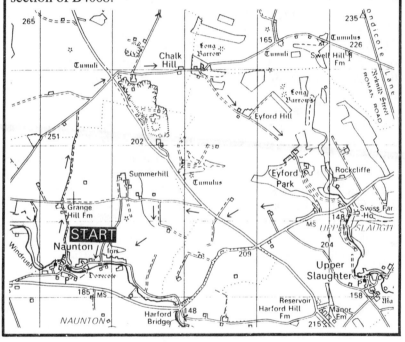

From standing with your back to the Black Horse Inn at Naunton, walk to the right for a few yards, then turn left to cross the Windrush. Turn right over the stone stile and walk with the river on the right. Notice the monkey-musk, no longer scented, growing in the stream; it is alleged that the scent was lost in the 1914-18 war and has never returned. Look out, too, for a Kingfisher which has been seen on many occasions.

When a track comes in from the right, continue straight ahead to

17

the road. Turn right, go over the river bridge and turn left at the fork. Follow this road uphill for ½ mile to Grange Hill Farm at the road junction. Cross the road and continue northwards, up a good track, for ¾ mile to a road. Turn right. In just under ½ mile go over the cross roads and continue ahead without deviation for ¾ mile to a road on the right marked "Private Road". It is, however, a bridle-way through Eyford Park.

This goes for 1¾ miles, becoming a grass track for a section. At the main road turn right and immediately right again and walk up the track, with some cottages on the left. Continue straight ahead through a gate. Follow the ascending track keeping to a wall on the left. Where the wall ends pass through a gate in the facing wall and continue in the same direction through 2 more fields along a definite track to a barn. Bear left along a track to the road.

Cross this and enter the track opposite. Immediately turn right so as to walk with a wall on the right and parallel with the road. (If this way is hopelessly muddy then it might be better to use the road.)

In about 270 yards follow the track as it bears left still parallel with the road. In just less than ½ mile a definite farm track is arrived at. Go down this. Go past a farm track on the left to continue for a few more yards, on a waymarked track, to the bottom of the descent. Here go right along a bridle track, pass through some trees and shrubs and continue over three fields to enter a coppice. Through the coppice, go along a good track into Naunton.

NAUNTON, RIVER WINDRUSH,
LOWER SLAUGHTER, UPPER SLAUGHTER,
SWISS FARM

A varied ramble with typical Cotswold villages and a beautiful section of the best known stream of the Cotswolds.
Map OS 163 in the 1:50,000 series.
Starting point: Grid reference 120235 Naunton.
Distance 9 miles.

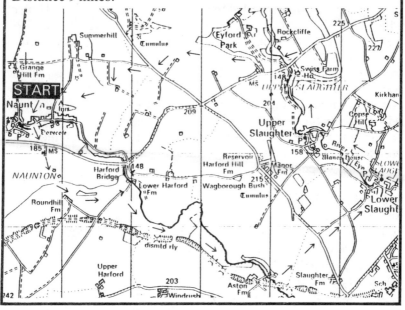

From the Black Horse Inn at Naunton walk westwards (i.e. in the direction of the Church) for a few yards and go into the first opening on the left. Cross the Windrush, and immediatley turn right over a stone stile to go along a path with the river on the right.

Notice the monkey musk already mentioned on page 17. also look out for the kingfisher which has been seen on several occasions. In about 250 yards there is a track on the right which crosses the river back into the village. At this point, turn up the slope on the left to a sunken trackway. Follow this to the road B4068. Cross and go along the signposted trackway opposite. In 350 yards pass a track on the left going to Lodges Barn.

Go ahead and pass through a gate. Now veer left and descend to

19

a brook. Cross the footbridge consisting of a single stone, turn left and immediately go through a gate. Go ahead with a stream on the left. Continue along the valley and in ½ mile pass over a waymarked stile and on to the road at Lower Harford.

Go through the gate opposite and follow the path to the River Windrush. Look out for Kingfishers and Herons.

Follow the river for 1¼ miles passing through 2 gateways and then a bridlegate with a waymark. Follow the waymarked path as it ascends diagonally right across a hilly field partially covered with gorse. At the top of the ascent, where there is a waymarked post, turn right. Continue ahead alongside a wood, stone wall and fence, which is on the left to a waymarked gate. Go through into a wood and follow the ascending track. Follow this definite track, often very very muddy, up and down through the wood until it emerges into the open at a waymark. Go in the direction indicated by the waymark to Aston Farm seen ahead. Walk through the yard of Aston Farm following the waymarks. At the subsidiary road turn left and cross the Windrush in front of Aston Mill House. With any requisite permission it is interesting to go into the open building (? garage) on the left of the house where will be seen the old mill race. The water wheel has gone but the outline of its position can be seen.

Continue along a bridleway and turn left on reaching a hedge and bank. Pass through a gateway into a field with a hedge on the right; pass through another gate and then in 70 yards leave the main track to go through a gate into a field on the right. Follow the wall on the right for about 30 yards but where it turns right continue ahead to a gate seen on the opposite side of the field. Cross a subsidiary road and continue along a well-defined track opposite to reach another subsidiary road. Cross this and go down the opposite road into Lower Slaughter (4½ miles have now been walked).

Cross the River Eye and turn left to the mill. Just past the post office turn left along a passage between buildings. Go through a kissing gate and cross 4 fields with the river on the left to another kissing gate. In the next field veer left downhill towards the stream to pass a lake which is on the left. Go through a kissing gate, cross over the stream by a bridge, and proceed along a path through a shrubbery to the road at Upper Slaughter, turn left. Where there is an entrance to the hotel car park on the left, and where there is a farmyard on the right, turn right. this means the church is on the left. At the village school on the left do not continue to the stream but turn left. The stream is now on the right.

Continue along a bridleway passing through a field gateway and then a wicket gate. Keep a hedge and Cress Cottage on the right and go along a track which leads through a gateway into a wood. At the fork bear left still with the stream on the right to the main road B4068.

Turn left and in ¼ mile there is a row of cottages on the right; turn right along the rough track immediately on the right of the cottages. (Not the ascending one through Eyford Park). Just through a gate are two grass tracks. Take the one on the left, uphill, keeping to a wall which is on the left and continue through two fields to a barn. Pass immediately alongside the barn to a farm road. Turn left to the main road. Cross this and enter the track opposite. Immediately turn right so as to walk with a wall on the right and parallel with the road. (if this is hopelessly muddy then it might be better to use the road.)

In about 270 yards follow the track as it bears left; still parallel with the road. In just less than ½ mile a definite farm track is arrived at. Go left down this. Go past a farm track on the left to continue for a few more yards, on a waymarked track, to the bottom of the descent. Here go right along a bridle track, pass through some trees and shrubs and continue over three fields to enter a coppice.

Through the coppice, go along a good track to the road. Turn left into Naunton.

FORD, SLADE BARN, PINNOCK, TEMPLE GUITING

An attractive ramble on paths very seldom used.
Distance 4½ miles.
Map OS 163 in the 1:50,000 series.
Starting point: Grid reference 087293 village of Ford.
Ford is about 7 miles S.S.W. of Broadway.

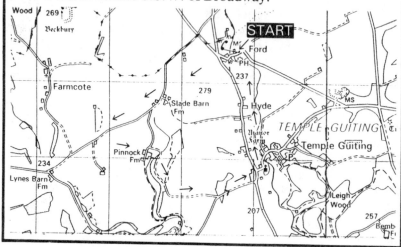

From the Plough Inn walk along B4077 with the Inn on the left. At the first crossroads turn left signposted Temple Guiting. In about 60 yards there is a gate on the right with a stone FP signpost. Go through the gate and turn immediately right into the adjoining field. Turn left and keep alongside the hedge which is on the left and ascend the field. In about 450 yards at a point where the way ahead is obstructed turn left through a signposted opening and then turn immediately right. Proceed ahead with a hedge on the right. In 250 yards where the hedge runs to the left, go through a gate in the growth on the right and go over a wire fence and enter a sunken track; go to the left and descend. At the farm buildings (Slade Barn) go through to the farm track and turn right to the road. Turn left.

In about ⅓ mile look for an opening in the hedge on the left which leads to a sunken track with a hedge on each side. As the entry to this path tends to get overgrown, some care may be required to locate it. Follow this track for about 450 yards to its entry into a field. Continue in the same direction, with a hedge on the right, to a field gate at a farm road (Pinnock Farm). Cross over, and follow the cartway down to where it crosses a tiny stream and continue ahead for a further ¾ mile to a T junction. Turn left and descend to a road. Turn left, and in a few yards go down a path on the right which descends to Temple Guiting Church. This village has associations with the Knights Templars and the church is 13th century (restored) with a 17th century tower. Turn right and cross over the bridge. On each side of the bridge there are ponds and you may see Muscovy ducks, moorhens and nuthatches and in the summer swallows and warblers.

After crossing the bridge take the first turn left and follow a path for about 500 yards with a hedge on the left and the Windrush below. When the path bends right, continue for a few yards beyond this bend and go through an opening on the left and continue with a hedge on the left and the Windrush below. In less than ½ mile, just before reaching the road, there is a bridle gate and a stile on the left. Go over the stile into a small rough field. Continue ahead making for the hedge on the right. Go through a gate in the hedge on to a piece of tarmacadam across the verge to the road. Turn left into Ford and the beginning of the walk.

FORD, CUTSDEAN, SCARBOROUGH FARM, FORDHILL FARM

Distance 6 miles.

Map OS 150 in the 1:50,000 series.

Starting point: Grid reference 087293. The village of Ford.

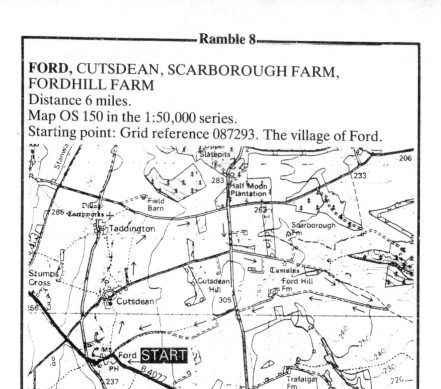

Looking to the left across the road from the Plough Inn, there is a wicket gate at the bend of the road. Go through. There may be no visible footpath but go across two fields making gradually for the bottom of the valley on the left. The general direction is towards Cutsdean seen ahead. Drop down to a kissing gate through which a stream flows in wet weather. From here bear right up the hill to the diagonal corner to another kissing gate.

Turn left along a hedge which is followed by a wall. Go past the church, which is on the left, to a gate leading to a road in Cutsdean. Turn right.

In approximately 50 yards past a house named Larks Rise turn left up a track. The track bears right at the top. Go through the gate in front. Turn left immediately and walk with the hedge on the left. Pass through two gates. After the second gate continue ahead along a wire fence. Where this fence turns sharp left continue ahead, bearing slightly right to the facing hedge to a point where there is a piece of wooden fencing. Go over this into the sunken lane. (In the field in front there is a pond which is fed by a spring. This is the source of the River Windrush).

Turn right and in 700 yards a road is reached. Turn right. In approximately 600 yards turn left down the farm road.

In ½ mile leave the farm road when it goes left to Scarborough Farm and continue ahead down the track. in a further 600 yards pass a track on the left which goes to Cutsdean Lodge, an old barn. In a further 100 yards there are two gateways. Go through the right hand one. Continue with a wall on the left. In about 400 yards, where the wall begins to bear left and descends slightly there is a gate on the left. Leave the wall to bear right across the field on a compass bearing of 130°. (If a compass is not available then bear right to make an angle of about 30° with the wall on the left.) This leads to the ruins of Botany Barn. it may be that the ruins of Botany Barn will not be immediately found. If the walker gets to a wall and there is a farm road on the other side it means that a point has been reached to the right of Botany Barn. In this case turn left along the wall until the ruins of Botany Barn are seen. If on the other hand there is a field on the other side it means that a point has been reached to the left of Botany Barn. In that case follow the wall to the right until the ruins of Botany Barn are seen. Continue past these ruins so as to leave them on the left. Pass through a gateway to a farm track. Turn right very sharply to make an acute angle. There is now a wall on the right. Follow the definite track for one mile to Fordhill Farm. Turn left down the farm track and then turn right up the hill to the road. Cross the road to go up the track almost opposite to walk with a wall on the left.

This track takes a sharp left hand bend and this is the easiest way back to Ford. However, the right of way continues straight ahead across a field to drop through some bushes into another field, and on the left of a hedge to rejoin the track. Bear right and go straight down to Ford and the beginning of the walk.

SNOWSHILL, SHENBERROW

An interesting village with a National Trust manor house.
Fine views over two valleys and an ancient British Fort of
considerable dimensions.
Distance 5½ miles.
Map OS 150 in 1:50,000 series.
Starting point: Grid reference 097337. The village of Snowshill.

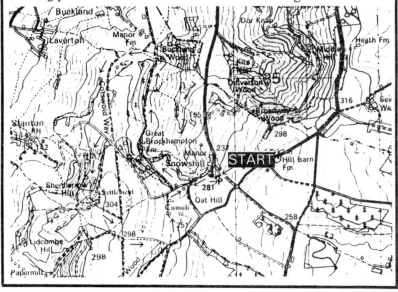

Snowshill is two miles south of Broadway. Snowshill Manor is a
National Trust property, open to the public, which has pleasant
gardens and an interesting museum.

Snowshill Arms Inn provides good refreshment in a pleasant
atmosphere.

Leave the village with the Snowshill Arms on the right, and the
Church on the left. Bearing right along the uphill road take the first
road on the right. In a further 250 yards, take a road on the right.
Walk 1¼ miles without deviation (passing to the left of Great Brockhampton Farm) with a wood on the left and the valley with good
views on the right. Pass through a gate. (Buckland Wood is on the
right.) Leave the road immediately and go diagonally left over a
knoll, drop to a track on the right and continue ahead with a fence
on the right.

Down below in the valley is the village of Buckland. At a gate with some blackberry bushes on the right, go up the track ahead. Continue straight ahead leaving Laverton Hill Barn away on the left.

Pass through a gate into a wood. When the path forks take the main one which is on the right. This leads to a rough road. Turn left and in a few yards go through the gate, with a cattle grid, on the right.

Continue up the farm road for about 800 yards to some grass mounds which are part of the site of an Ancient British Fort.

Go through the gate on the left (SP Bridleway). Follow the track through the farm buildings and continue along the ascending stone track with a wall on the right.

At a T junction with another farm track turn right. After passing through a bridle gate there are cross tracks. Immediately turn left and descend to the road. Here turn left and immediately go through a gate on the left. With a hedge and then a fence close on the left continue across the field to a gate. Go through, and continue ahead with a fence on the right. Pass to the left of some farm buildings and follow the track to the road. Turn right and go straight ahead.

In less than ½ mile Snowshill is reached.

SNOWSHILL, SNOWSHILL HILL

A varied walk.
Distance 5½ miles.
Map OS 150 in the 1:50,000 series.
Starting point: Grid reference 097337. The village of
Snowshill which is about two miles south of Broadway.

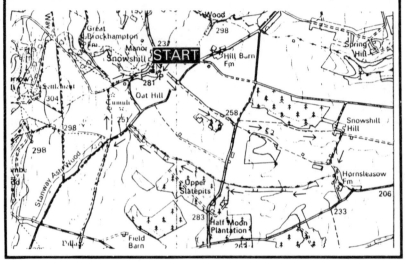

Starting from Snowshill, walk with the inn on the right and the
church on the left. In a few yards, turn left up the hill with the
church still on the left.

At the crossroads, turn right, go over the next crossroads, and
continue for a little over half a mile to a T junction. Here turn left
and in about 75 yards go through the gate on the right. Follow the
clear grass track over four fields to Snowshill Hill Farm and manor
house. Go through the farmyard and turn right down the hill along
the metalled road.

Cross the first cattle grid and go past a farm cottage with a sign
on the side indicating it was constructed in 1878 and reconstructed
in 1971. Continue down the hill with conifers on the left for just
over 200 yards past this cottage and go through a wall by what used
to be a gateway with farm buildings about 150 yards ahead. 20 yards
after passing through this old gateway turn sharp right along a
raised bank to cross a field bounded by 3 stone walls. Go through
a wicket gate. Walk ahead with a wall on the left and an open field

on the right; continue ahead over some hummocky ground which appears to have been quarried. Pass through a sparse wood to a gate, and go ahead across a large field with the wall still on the left.

This leads to the road. Crossing the road, go through a gate opposite. With Upper Slate Pits wood on the left, cross the first field to a gate, go through, cross the farm track and continue in the same direction, keeping the wood on the left. Go over two more fields. The fencing may vary a little according to the needs of farming but it is possible to distinguish that which is only temporary. At the end of the second of these two fields, an opening leads into the wood on the left, with a very definite track. Follow this, and in 50 yards come out into the open on the far side of the wood which is known as Welshman's Hedge Plantation. The track now reached is probably one of the old drovers' roads along which, for generations, sheep and cattle were driven. Turn right.

In 450 yards, on reaching the road, turn left. About 250 yards further on the road forks. Just before the division there are two gates on the right. Take the one on the right and proceed over the field for roughly 300 yards, keeping the hedge on the left, until a gate is reached. Pass through and continue in the same direction with the hedge now on the right. Keep to the left of some farm buildings, and having reached the road, turn right and go straight ahead. In less than half a mile Snowshill is reached.

HORNLEASOWS QUARRY, HINCHWICK

This walk is well worth while just for the lovely valley from
Hornleasows Quarry to Hinchwick.

Distance 7 miles.

Map OS 150 & 151 in the 1:50,000 series.

Starting point: Grid reference 130322. A disused quarry
2½ miles west of Bourton-on-the-Hill and 2 miles east south
east of Snowshill.

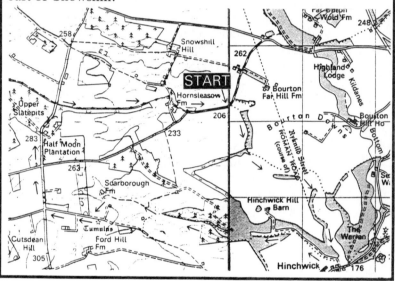

To reach the starting point from Broadway, take the A44 Oxford
road up Fish Hill. Continue for five miles to where th A424 forks
off to the right to Stow-on-the-Wold. Follow the A424 and in 200
yards take the road on the right (signposted Snowshill). In about a
mile bear left up the hill (SP Bourton on the Water and Stow-on-
the-Wold). In half a mile, just before the bottom of a descent there
is a quarry on the left. This is the start of the ramble.

Continue down the road: at the lowest point of the curve, below
the quarry turn left to leave the road along a definite track to pass
into a copse. On emerging from the copse into an open area, at the
foot of the quarry, continue ahead to pass to the right of a detached
wall. In a few yards at a fork bear right along a descending track.
Cross the end of a track which descends from the left to continue
ahead through the wood with a wall on the right for 500 yards to the

end of the wood. Follow the wall for a further quarter of a mile to where the boundaries of four fields meet. Turn right through a wicket gate into the adjoining field and then immediately left to continue down the enchanting valley for a little over a mile.

At the end of the wood on the right, with Hinchwick seen in front, do a complete right about turn, round the end of the wood, to go along a farm road, with the wood now on the right.

Follow this road for ½ mile and at a sort of rough layby on the right and 100 yards before the road sweeps up to the right, leave the road to bear left down a green track into the valley bottom, keeping to the edge of the wood on the right. In a few yards the path forks: take the left hand one. Continue along the valley bottom with the edge of the wood on the right. At a conjunction of tracks, with a farm road sweeping up to the right, continue straight ahead along the green track, still along the valley bottom. The track rises to the disused farmstead — Cutsdean Lodge. Bear left and in 175 yards a well defined track is reached. Turn right and pass the entrance of Scarborough Farm which is on the right and continue for a further ½ mile to the road.

Turn right. In 600 yards pass Half Moon Plantation which is on the right. Continue along the road for a further 1000 yards to the end of Upper Slatepits Plantation which is on the left. Immediately at the end of this plantation, on the right hand side of the road, there is a wicket gate to a field on the right. Go through this gate and follow the wall and wood on the right. In less than ½ mile go through a wicket gate into a thinly-treed wood.

Continue with the wall on the right and in just over another ½ mile pass through a wicket gate and cross a small pasture to a road. Turn right.

Pass a cattle grid which is on the right and continue ahead down the green track with Hornleasows Farm on the right.

In 300 yards go throught the gate on to the road.

Turn left. In ¼ mile the quarry is reached from which the walk started.

STANWAY, STANTON, SHENBERROW, LIDCOMBE WOOD

This walk includes two charming villages, a short section of the Cotswold Way, an ancient British Camp, a ridge with long distance views, and an interesting wood.
Distance 4½ miles.
Map OS 150 in the 1:50,000 series.
Starting point: Grid reference 060322. The village of Stanway.

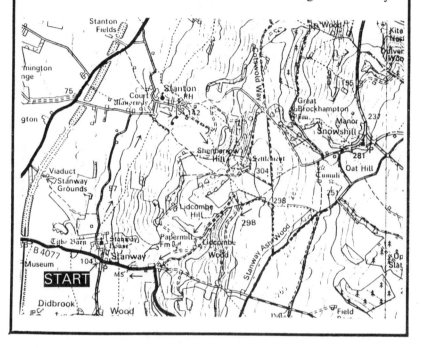

Before leaving the village, look at the stone gateway to Stanway House. It is very beautiful and is reputed to have been designed by Inigo Jones.

Walk with this gateway and the church on the right, to pass some reconstructed cottages on the left. The interest in these cottages is set out on a notice-board alongside. In a further 100 yards the Tithe barn of Stanway House is seen on the right. This is not open to the general public except on special occasions. Special permission is required but this is available for anyone interested in forming a party. In a further 60 yards the drive to Stanway House is seen on the right. There is a good view of this beautiful house of the Wemys family. In a further 150 yards there is a signpost to Stanton and a stile on the right. Go over and walk diagonally to the left to another stile.

From here the way to Stanton is indicated by the Cotwold Way sign (a white spot and a yellow arrow) and also by some coloured green posts. It will probably make it easier to follow with the following additional directions.

In the next field continue in the same direction making for a belt of trees. A barn will be seen on the left. Keep to the right of this barn to a group of seven oak trees, and continue to the fence. Go over the stile with the Cotswold Way sign. Then walk diagonally left through three sycamore trees to a gate. Go through this gate, and skirt a mound leaving seven oak trees on the left. From the gate take the direction indicated by a green post and continue to a second green post. Walk with a fence about 50 yards away on the left to a gap in the hedge in front. Cross the stile. Continue in the same direction with a fence on the left about 70 yards away. Continuing, bear to the right so that on reaching the hedge in front, the hedge on the left is about 200 yards away. Cross the stile with a Cotswold Way marking. Cross two fields to another stile. Go over the next field making for a point immediately to the right of the farm buildings seen ahead. At the farm road, turn left and then at the road turn right, to walk through the gracious village of Stanton.

At the next fork, turn right up the village, and at the following one turn right again. (The left fork goes up to the Mount Inn which is worth a visit for the pleasant view from its terrace.) Continue to a gateway and take the road which is marked Shenberrow. In about 600 yards, just before a gate and two enormous cylinders, turn down to the right as indicated by the Cotswold Way sign, through some rough grass. Ascend a narrow track to a wicket gate.

Through this bear right to skirt a pond which is on the right. At the bottom of the slope follow the hedge on the right to a broken gate. Go through and ascend with a wall and fence on the left for about 100 yards past a hydraulic ram to a stile/fence. Pass over this stile/fence. Go ahead for a few yards and then turn up the valley to the right, continuing to the trees on Shenberrow Hill with some cottages about 60 yards to the left.

(Away to the right about 200 yards away a wicket gate will be seen in a wall but there is no right of way.)

Walk to the left of the cottages up a stony track to a gate on the right. Go through along the indicated bridleway. Follow this round through the farm buildings. At the end of these buildings do not follow the main track to the left but continue ahead so as to walk with a wall and spinney on the right. Go through the first gate on the right and then go diagonally left to the wicket gate seen in the wall. This is the gate referred to in the brackets above. Go through the wicket gate and immediately turn left and walk with a wall on the left.

At the end of the field, go through a gate into a wood and walk along a rough cartway for about 400 yards to a point where there is a signpost on the left indicating the way to Shenberrow. At this point turn right with a wood on the right, and go through a gate into a wood. Continue downhill along the bridleway following signs without any deviation to the road B4077 at a strong bend. To the left it goes up Stanway Hill, but turn right down the road. Just before a house known as the Old Bakehouse, (which supplies refreshment) take a signposted path on the right. When the path forks take the track to the right passing to the right of a timber yard. Follow this track into Stanway.

BOURTON FAR HILL FARM, FAR UPTON WOLD, BLOCKLEY, DOVEDALE, BOURTON DOWNS
Distance 7 miles.
Map OS 151 in the 1:50,000 series.
Starting point: Grid reference 132327.

To reach the starting point from Broadway, take the A44 going up Fish Hill. About 5 miles out, at a fork with A44 and A424 take A424 to the right. In 200 yards, at the first crossroads, turn right. In just over a mile, at a fork, bear left. In a further 500 yards Smallthorns Farm is on the right, and the drive to Bourton Far Hill Farm on the left. This is the start of the walk.

Go up the drive of Bourton Far Hill Farm. Pass through a gate at the approach to the farm and after a few yards with the farmhouse on the right turn left through a gate and follow a wall on the left. Continue through two gates and then descend to a gate on the road. Turn right for 200 yards, then turn left at the entrance to Far Upton Wold.

Follow this roadway to the Jockey Stable Cottages. Near the last cottage on the right, cross over the cattle grid, turn sharp right for a few yards then sharp left and with the stream on the left follow it by an ill-defined footpath across a field towards the woods ahead. Continue past the pond on the left, pass through a gate and follow the footpath alongside the wall which encloses a coppice on the right. With coppices on each side continue ahead and pass through a gate to join a bridle road which ascends gradually to the main road ahead, which is the Five Mile Drive.

Cross the road, turn right for about 20 yards, then left to join a bridle road opening into a coppice fringing the road.

Follow the footpath across the field. If the path has become indefinite then go across the field, with the hedge on each side about equidistant, to the gap in the facing hedge.

Continue across the next field in approximatley the same direction to a gap in the facing boundary wall. Now follow on with, a hedge on the left, to Warren Farm.

A definite farm track now leads to a road coming in from the left. Continue ahead to a road and turn left into Blockley which offers a choice to two inns (2½ miles have now been walked).

From Blockley walk back along the road just traversed (past the point where the cart track joined the road) to enter Dovedale, where the metalled road merges into a cart track with woodland on each side. Follow this well defined track, past the pumping station and with Bourton Wood on the left, without deviating until it joins the Five Mile Drive A44 at Trooper's Lodge. Here turn left.

At the junction of A44 and A424 go along the A424. In about 200 yards, go over a cross roads. Continue along the A424 for 600 yards to another crossroads. Turn right. In 250 yards a track forks to the right. Take this to descend past Bourton Hill House which is on the right. Just beyond Bourton Hill House the road merges into a rough bridle track. Continue along this track without deviation for ¾ mile to where it begins to descend and Bourton Hill Farm can be seen on the right. Continue to descend with a wall on the right until this farm is at a right angle with the track. At this point go through the gate on the right and proceed with a wall which is succeeded by a fence on the left. Follow this as it encloses the farm. Do not go through any of the gates until the farm is immediately on the left at the end of the field. Pass through this gate and go ahead down the farm drive to the beginning of the walk.

BLOCKELY, EDGE OF DOVEDALE, NORCOMBE WOOD,

Pleasant woodland walking with a richness of flora.
Distance 3½ miles.
Map OS 151 in the 1:50,000 series.
Starting point: Grid reference 164349. The village of Blockley.

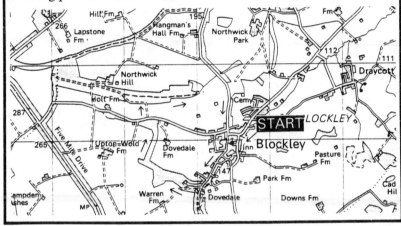

With the Crown Hotel on the right go down the street to the end of the village. Vine Cottage is on the right. Immediately past this cottage take the track on the right. In 150 yards at a fork go to the right. Pass a house which is on the right and then go over a stile to the left of a gate with a notice about the Northwick Estate. Continue up the main track through the wood without deviation to the road. Cross the road and continue along the track opposite. At the T junction turn right along a definite ascending bridle track. Continue ahead without deviation to descend to a gate. Go up the ascent in front to the junction of the fence ahead with one on the left. Go over the fence on the left, and walk with a fence on the right to a stile on the right. Go diagonally left across the football field to the road and turn right to descend into Blockley.

WINCHCOMBE, LANGLEY HILL, NOTTINGHAM HILL, POSTLIP

Good views from Langley Hill and a pleasant descent to near Postlip Hall and then a woodland walk.
Distance 8 miles.
Map OS 163 in the 1:50,000 series.
Starting point: Grid reference 025283. Winchcombe.

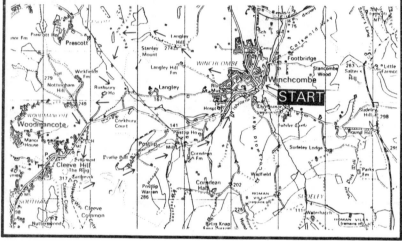

From the car park in the centre of Winchcombe turn right along the road towards Broadway and then immediately turn left up the road opposite the Methodist Church. In about 200 yards take the footpath on the left to pass the new library and clinic which is on the left. At the road turn left and take the second turn on the right (Barnmeadow Road) and go to the end of the T junction. Here turn left up Orchard Road and at the end of the road turn right along a track to a signpost "Langley Hill 1 Mile". Go over the stile and cross the field towards the farm buildings seen ahead. Go through a gate and continue towards the farm buildings. Just before the farm buildings go over the stile, veer right, and in 10 yards go over another stile and a tiny brook. Bear left uphill. There are two gates ahead. Go through the left hand one and continue up the steep slope to the top of a very long field.

Go over the stile, with a Wychavon Way marking, a yellow W and an arrow, in the top right hand corner of the field. Go to the wall opposite, turn left and follow the wall which is on the right.

Ignore tracks on the left which lead to the summit of Langley Hill.

Where the track forks take the definite track to the left (not the one on the right leading through a gate into a field) and follow this track, with Wychavon Way signs, below the wooded slopes on the left. Pass through a gate and continue to follow the signs but 60 yards before a bridle gate leave the Wychavon Way to pass through this bridle gate. Go ahead with the wood still on the left for ¼ mile of rough ground. When the wood ends continue for a further 200 yards to a stone wall. Bear right downhill along a fence and a line of small trees. At the bottom of the field go through a gate on the left. Go ahead (ignore the gate on the left) for 60 yards to another gate. Pass through into a track with trees on both sides and a fence on the left. On arriving at two gates go through the right hand one.

Where the trees finish on the left continue ahead following a fence on the right for a few yards to a gate which pass through, veer slightly left, and in 30 yards pass through another gate. Now follow the hedge on the left to a small barn under some power lines. Immediately turn right to descend with a fence on the right.

Go through the bridle gate at the bottom of the field. Turn left and walk with the wood on the left. When the wood ends go through a gate and continue in the same direction over two fields towards a house. Near the house go through a gate on the left on to the road.

Turn right and in 30 yards go over the stile on the right. This brings the walker into the same field just left but the description follows the right of way.

Go straight ahead up the field towards the left hand of two buildings, seen at the top of the ascent, crossing a fence and a 5-bar gate in the intervening hedges. Pass through a single gate on to a track, immediately in front of a pair of cottages, and turn left.

Almost immediately turn right and go through a gate and follow a fence on the right for 60 yards to the corner. Go over the wall (it is easier to go through the gate in this wall but it isnot the right of way) and bear left to about half way along the facing wall. (If you have gone through the gate in the wall then follow the wall on the left to the same point). Go over the stile in this wall. Turn right and follow the wall. At the corner bear left continuing to follow the wall to the end of the field. Cross the stile into a definite track and in a few yards at a road turn left and walk to the main road A46.

Cross the road and go up the one opposite. Near the Golf House which is on the right, go through the gate (Cleeve Hill). Cross the tracks going right and left and go straight ahead. In a few yards the track forks: take the track to the left. In about 700 yards there is a concrete garage on the right. 500 yards beyond this there is a junction of about 7 tracks the one on the left obviously leading down into a valley. Continue ahead for about 500 yards to where the rubble track merges into a green track. Take a descending green track on the left. In 70 yards at a junction of tracks take the second on the left i.e. avoiding the descending one. In a little while the track begins to drop. Do not go into the valley on the right but continue on the left hand side of the valley with the scar of an old quarry on the other side. Winchcombe comes into view slightly to the right. Continue the descent through some quarry workings to the circular wood seen ahead. Descend to the wood and go over the fence into the wood. Now follow the footpath markings to the iron roofed barn. Leave the barn on the right and in a few yards turn right through a gate between a high wall and another barn. Follow the wall and go through a bridle gate following a path with the wall still on the left.

Go through a gate and cross a track (with Postlip Hall on the left) into a spinney opposite via a stile with a footpath sign to Winchcombe. Follow the path with a fence on the right and a stream on the left. Go over a stile and pass to the left of a barn and go over another stile. Go along the edge of the field with a hedge on the left. Pass over a stile into another field. Go along with the hedge on the left and at the end of the field go through the hedge and cross the concrete slab over the tiny stream.

Turn right along a track with the stream now on the right go through the car park ahead into the paper mill yard.

Leave the mill fire station on the right to ascend to a road at a T junction. Turn right and descend into the mill yard. (This is somewhat circuitous but it seems to follow the right of way). At the mill yard turn left. Go ahead keeping alongside some open storage buildings on the left. Continue ahead for about 300 yards to pass through a kissing gate. In a further 150 yards the road bears left. Here go straight ahead over a stile and follow a fence which is on the right. Cross three fields and emerge on to the road on the outskirts of Winchcombe.

WINCHCOMBE, MONK'S HOLE
A ramble with splended views.
Distance 3 miles.
Map OS 163 in the 1:50,000 series.
Starting point: Grid reference 025283. Winchcombe.

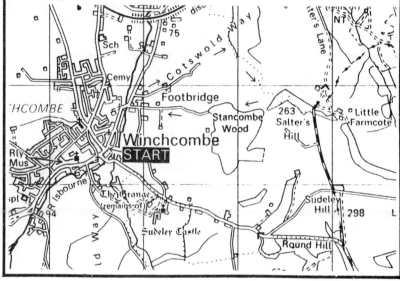

From the car park in the centre of Winchcombe, walk along the A46 in the direction of Broadway, so as to leave the Methodist Church and George Hotel on the right. Continue down the hill and over the River Isbourne and take the second turn on the right at a house called Hayles Way. This lane is called Puck Pit Lane. Follow it bearing right at a signpost "Hailes Abbey 2 Km". Follow this track to where it ends. Ignore the gate on the right and continue up the field ahead, as indicated by the Cotswold Way sign, with a hedge on the right and a fence on the left. In about 50 yards cross a stile and then bear diagonally left across the field towards an old barn with a corrugated iron roof. If there is any difficulty in locating this barn then make for the hedge on the left and ascend with it on the left. About 40 yards below the barn go through a gap into the next field. Turn right to pass the barn which is now on the right. Just past the barn turn left to follow a hedge which is now on the right. Continue to the end of the field; turn left for about 25 yards. Go through the gate with a Cotswold Way sign.

Turn diagonally right to a thin line of trees and ascend with these on the right. Pass through a gate and follow a ditch and a line of trees forming a hedge. When the line of trees finishes proceed ahead ascending steeply towards a clump of trees on a knoll, leaving them about 80 yards to the right so as to arrive at a gate in a facing wall. Do not go through the gate but turn sharp right up the steep ascent, with the wall on the left, towards the trees on the knoll. At a fence before the summit turn right and in about 30 yards go over the stile on the left. In a few yards go over a fence and then through a circle of trees. This is Monks Hole on the side of Salters Hill.

Follow a wall which is on the left.

In about 60 yards pass a bridle gate (do not go through) follow the definite descending track for 130 yards. At this point there is a gate on the left. Do not go through but turn half right and descend to a bridle gate in the boundary of the field.

Pass into the next field and turn left. Continue near to the left boundary of this field to a wood. Turn right and descend with the wood on the left. Gradually move away from the wood to the right so as to arrive about 50 yards from it at a facing gate. Go over the gate.

Descend in the same direction but veer slightly left and go over a gate into a road.

Turn right and descend into Winchcombe.

PUESDOWN INN, HAZLETON, LOWER BARN, DOWNSBARN

A walk which takes in some unfrequented valleys.
Distance 5½ miles. This may be reduced to 4 miles by
starting from the village of Hazleton.
Map OS 163 in the 1:50,000 series.
Starting point: Grid reference 075172. The Puesdown Inn
on the A40(T) between Andoversford and Northleach. The inn
is about 5 miles from Northleach going towards Andoversford.

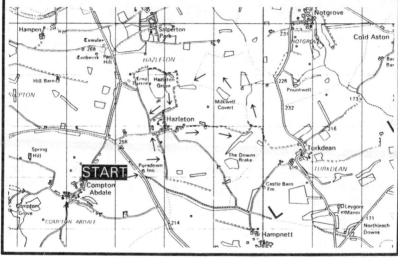

Face the Puesdown Inn, and go into the inn yard to the left of the
inn, and over a stile in the left hand corner, ignoring any obstructions. Walk through one field with the wall on the left, a distance
of about 500 yards. At the rough lane turn left and walk ½ mile to
the subsidiary road at Hazleton.

Turn right and, going downhill; ignore the roads to the left. Fork
left down the narrow road marked "Unsuitable for Motors". At
the end of this road follow the track ahead for 1¼. This 1¼ miles
leads through 3 metal gates.

A few yards beyond the third metal gate the path forks; the left
one rising up the hill side. Follow the right hand one along the valley bottom to a wooden gate. Go through and immediately turn left
through a metal gate.

Continue along the valley bottom, with its satisfying contours,

43

for ¾ mile. Go through the first gate on the left at a point where there is a crossing of the tiny stream. Follow the track through the rough pasture rising gradually to Down Barn which is immediately to the left of the wood seen ahead.

From now on the narrative should be followed very carefully.

At the barn turn left for 350 yards, with a wall on the left, to the top of a slight incline.

At this point it is possible by looking diagonally to the right to see the corner of the field. Walk diagonally to the right to that corner, go over the wall and then immediately turn left through an iron gate.

Walk down the field on a compass bearing of 235° or, if a compass is not available, walk down the field at an angle of 45° to the wall on the left. Soon a spinney will appear in the valley below. Continue in the same direction making for the right hand side of the spinney to a gate in the facing fence. Pass through the gate and continue to the definite track at the bottom of the valley. Turn right, go through a gateway and continue along the definite track with a wood on the left. In about 500 yards follow the track uphill to the left. At the road continue to the church in the village of Hazleton.

Take the road on the left and at the next T junction turn right.

From here take the opposite way to that followed at the beginning of the walk.

PUESDOWN INN, COMPTON ABDALE, YANWORTH, HAMPNETT

What does one say about this ramble? Sufficient perhaps to say that its preparation and subsequent checking gave great pleasure.

Map OS 163 in the 1:50,000 series.

Distance 7½ miles.

Starting point: Grid reference 075172. The Puesdown Inn is on the A40(T) between Andoversford and Northleach. The inn is about 5 miles from Northleach going towards Andoversford.

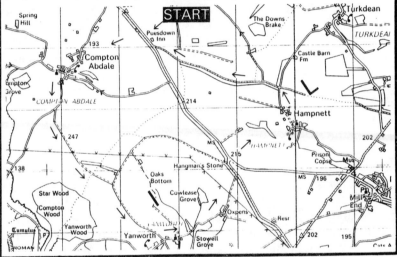

With the Puesdown Inn on the right walk for 200 yards along the A40. Cross the road and go through a gate immediately before the Honey Pot Restaurant.

Bear slightly right across a field to a gate in the facing wall. Go across a farm track and through the opposite gate. A line of cottages will be seen ahead slightly to the right. Go across the field towards these to arrive in the corner of the field at a gap and a stile. Go through and continue with a wall on the left to the end of a short road. Turn left into Compton Abdale.

At the crossroads continue ahead up the hill. Before doing so note the water spout on the right hand side in the form of a crocodile's head.

In 600 yards, as the road levels out at the top of the hill, on the left there is a double gate with a wicket gate and stile to the right of it. Go over the stile into the farm track and go ahead. At the junction with another track pass through a belt of trees on the right. The bridleway merges into a good farm track and descends into Yanworth.

Where the track meets a road turn left downhill towards the church passing some stone houses which are on the left. After the church follow the road around to the left between farm buildings and then right downhill into the valley.

Continue ahead as the road ascends. At the top of the ascent there is a wood on the right immediately alongside the road and a gate with a FP sign on the left. Go through this gate and walk diagonally right across a small field to a stile with a FP sign. Go over the stile and go along an enclosed path to a stile with a FP sign. Cross the stile into a farm track. Turn left and go through a farm gate and continue down the field to a facing gate with a FP sign.

Turn right and walk over 3 fields with the field boundary alongside on the left to a stile which pass over into a farm track: notice the Hangman's Stone. Turn right and at the minor road turn left to the main road.

Cross the road carefully and go through the right hand gate into the field keeping the stone wall to the left. Go over the stile in the corner of the field and continue downhill in the same direction. Cross a distinct bridleway and continue up the hill opposite in the same direction. A stone wall comes in on the left. Go through the gate with the wall and corner of the wood on the left. At the top of a short ascent bear left keeping a fence on the left. After the fence ends keep straight ahead to a gate opposite. Go through this to the road in a lovely village of Hampnett.

Turn left and follow the road to the right up the hill to the junction. (To visit the church continue ahead. The church has some unusual decorations. These were done in Victorian times and are not to all tastes). Turn left and go along the road to the A40. Cross the road (traffic dangerous) and go up the road opposite. In about 70 yards take the road on the left signposted Hazleton. In about 350 yards, where the road turns right go straight ahead up an unsignposted enclosed track. This can be very muddy but, although overgrown, is fairly definite. The enclosed track comes into the open; continue ahead along an indefinite track to the road A40.

Turn right to the Puesdown Inn and the end of the walk.

BROCKHAMPTON, SEVENHAMPTON, ANDOVERSFORD, SYREFORD

In this ramble there is a beautiful descent into the charming village of Sevenhampton.

Distance 5½ miles.

Map OS 163 in the 1:50,00 series.

Starting point: Grid reference 047220. ¾ mile east of Brockhampton at a T junction.

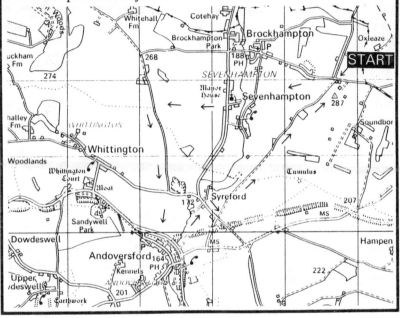

To reach the starting point from Winchcombe, take the Cheltenham road to the end of Winchcombe, then turn left along a road signposted Brockhampton on the left. Turn left into Brockhampton, and continue for ½ mile beyond the village to the first road on the left at the top of the hill. This is the start of the ramble.

Go back down towards Brockhampton for 300 yards. At the first house on the left, which is at the bottom of a bank, go through the gate on the left by the wall of the house. Skirt the wall and trees on the right and in a few yards go over a stile in the wall. Continue westerly along the tree lined fence on the right towards Sevenhampton which can be seen below. In the second field bear left (i.e. S.W.)

47

and go over a stile in the fence ahead. Keep the same direction over a field to a stile in a wall. Over the stile, turn left and follow the wall round the right angle to a convenient crossing place about 150 yards from the corner. then turn diagonally right, and go almost due west to the first building seen below. (This is the old school now made into a private house). Go over the stile, cross the road and go over the stile opposite. Follow the track which goes over a stone footbridge and up the other side to a road. this is Sevenhampton and do not hurry through it.

Continue to the road at the T junction. Cross the road and go through the gate opposite and continue with the wall on the left for 500 yards. Pass through the gate straight ahead, and then walk with the wall on the right for ½ mile to the road. Turn left, and follow this for a mile to another road. Cross this and go down the bridle way straight ahead. At the main road A40(T) cross over (traffic dangerous) and go straight ahead down a rough road through a yard to a road. This is Andoversford. 3½ miles have now been walked. Refreshment is available in this village.

Turn left and a few yards before the Andoversford Hotel turn left on a track through a yard. Go through a tunnel to the main road A40(T). Cross (traffic dangerous) and go along the metalled track ahead.

With the sewage works on the left and a hedge on the right go along the track (this can be overgrown with nettles so take a stick) to the old railway embankment. Turn right and in a few yards go through a dismantled railway arch on the left.

Cross the field along a path which will be about 35 yards from the brook and hedge which is on the left. In about 200 yards at a large tree the hedge on the left comes round near the path. At this point leave the path and go into the wood through an opening. This opening gets very overgrown so it may not be easy to locate. Once having found it there is a clear path through the wood to a private road (with a public right of way for walkers).

Turn right and walk to the road at Syreford. Turn right and in 250 yards at a fork bear left. Almost immediately take a bridleway on the left. Follow this keeping to the wall on the left for 1½ miles to the beginning of the ramble,

FROGMILL INN (near Andoversford), FOXCOTE,
PEGGLEWORTH HILL, WITHINGTON,
UPCOTE FARM, THORNDALE
A ramble with extensive views from Peggleworth Hill.
Distance 7½ miles.
Map OS 163 in the 1:50,000 series.
Starting point: Grid reference 027183. At or near the Frogmill
Inn.

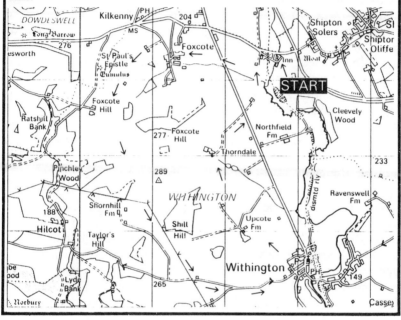

The Frogmill Inn is about 5 miles south east of Cheltenham and
1 mile south of Andoversford. It is in a loop taken off the A436 in
the section which goes towards Northleach. Morning coffee and
other refreshments are served at the Inn.

If the start is made from the Inn, walk back over the railway
bridge to A436. Immediately at A436 turn left down a bridle way
which is metalled at the beginning. Pass through a gate and in a few
yards at a storage barn take a path immediately to the right of it.
This means walking at a right-angle to the bridle road just left. If
the path becomes at all doubtful then check the direction by walking parallel to a hedge which is on the right.

On reaching a hedge making a right-angle continue ahead on a definite track alongside a hedge on the right to the end of the field. Pass through an opening onto the road. Go through a gate on the opposite side a few yards to the right into a field. Go ahead alongside a hedge/fence which is on the right. At the end of this field there is a wicket gate and stile. Pass into the next field and continue alongside a fence on the right. At the end of this field pass over a gate in the beginning of Foxcote village. Immediately turn right and go alongside the right hand side of a wall. Go through a yard and some farm buildings, pass the left of a house into a wide definite track. In about 200 yards just at the end of some farm buildings where the track swings to the right go through a wicket gate on the left.

Follow a hedge which is on the left, go through a gate and straight across an avenue of trees, then take the bridle way straight ahead. At the next road cross over and go along the bridle road opposite and continue past a barn on the right and some piggeries on the left. Continue to another gate which gives access to a rising open field. Follow the very definite track. As it levels out continue ahead to a stone wall. Here turn left along a definite farm track. Follow alongside a wall which is on the right for ½ mile at a point near some power lines and go through the gate straight ahead.

Go on with a wall now on the left, and following a line of pylons. Descend to a gate and go into a rough rising field. Bear slightly left across a field and pass a waterhole which is on the right and still following a line of pylons to arrive at a wall on the left. Continue in the same direction to the corner of the field. Go through a gate; on passing through the gate follow a bridle way, with a line of trees on the right. (The Ordnance Survey Map may show a different direction for the path but there has been a legal diversion).

Where the bridle way makes a T junction with a rough road with a gate a few yards to the left, turn right. In ¼ mile a subsidiary road is reached. Turn left, and walk into Withington. The Mill Inn is down through the village.

Starting at the Inn and walking northwards i.e. towards the church but not as far, take the first turn left, and then the next turn right. Continue over the crossroads and follow the sunken bridle road through a spiney. On emerging from the spinney continue in the same direction with a hedge on the right for ½ mile through Upcote Farm. Keep straight ahead through the farmyard, passing two cart tracks on the right, and at the next fork with a fence on the right for 1½ miles to Thorndale. Here, bear right, and continue along the farm track to the road. Cross the road, and walk along the opposite bridleway to Fulford Farm. Follow the farm wall on the left to the continuing bridleway and so to the main road. Turn right to the Frogmill Inn and the end of the ramble.

RIVER COLN, CHEDWORTH WOODS,

A bright ramble along a beautiful river and through pleasant woods and then along a ridge with good views.

Distance 4 miles.

Map OS 163 in the 1:50,000 series.

Starting point: Grid reference 072130 alongside the River Coln.

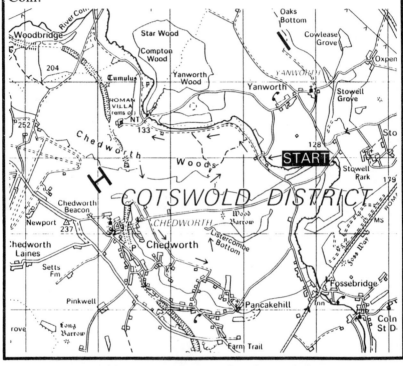

The starting point of the ramble may by approached from Yanworth which is about 2 miles west of Northleach. At the west end of the village of Yanworth take the road on the left going south. In 650 yards pass an old mill, which has been converted into a house, and cross the River Coln. In a few yards further, where the road turns sharply to the left, there is a private road on the right which runs parallel to the river but which is about 80 yards away.

This is the start of the ramble.

Go along this private road with the Chedworth Wood on the left for just over 1 mile. At the junction with the road turn left and in

100 yards take the bridleway on the left (not the one to the National Trust car park) to enter the woods.

In about 50 yards at a fork go left and pass through a gate. Continue ahead ascending with an overgrown stone wall on the left. On emerging from the wood go ahead, still with the wall on the left, to the corner of the field. Do not go over the stile in front, which provides a descent into the valley, but bear slightly left to go through a gate onto a track. Proceed past a stone farm building and pass through a gate into a farm track.

Cross a road and go along the track ahead. In about a mile there is a descending metalled farm track on the right which goes to Greenhill Farm. Here turn left as indicated by a footpath sign. This sign and a number following have been erected by Mr. John Shedden, Greenhill Farm Chedworth, to whom we are indebted.

Follow the hedge which is on the left and at the end of this field pass into the next field through a gate on the right which is signposted. Go down this narrow field and at the bottom pass through a signposted gate on the right. Bear left as indicated by the sign, go down the steep descent into Listercombe Bottom and up the other side to a wicket gate. Pass through and bear left through dense growth to hedge on the left to pass through a wicket gate. At this point the description is a departure from the right of way but is approved by Mr. John Shedden.

Follow the path as it ascends through dense growth. When the track forks take the ascending one on the right to arrive at a definite track. Go along this track alongside a wall on the right to the road (We took this clear track because of growing crops in the field on the right; but to get to the right of way on coming to the definite track, referred to above, turn into the field on the right and walk for about 60 yards alongside a hedge on the right then turn sharp left across the field to walk parallel with the wall on the left. Go over a stone stile, cross the road, and go through the gate opposite into a field).

Turn right and in about 90 yards locate a stone stile on the right. Go through a gate opposite into a field.

Follow a compass bearing from this gate of 28°. This will mean walking parallel to and about 40 yards from the wall on the left, towards the wood ahead. Keep the same direction making for a point where the wood protrudes into the field. Descend with part of the wood immediately on the right. At the bottom of the descent turn right into the wood and follow the track going slightly downhill. The track passes to the left of some tall conifers. Where these end, a track comes in on the right and at this point fork left along a faint track rising for about 30 yards. Bear right on meeting the next track and follow this for another 30 yards. Here the track forks. Take the left fork and ignore the track immediately to the left. After another 30 yards the track appears to end where it meets a path to the left and right. Ignore this track and keep straight ahead into the bracken and undergrowth, and bearing very slightly left all the time until a faint track is discerned. Follow this steeply down to the road and to the beginning and end of the walk.

Ramble 22, Cooper's Hill

Ramble 22

GRANHAM CORNER, COOPER'S HILL, CRANHAM

Distance 3½ miles.
Maps OS 162 & 163 in the 1:50,000 series.
Starting point: Grid reference 882130. Prinknash Corner.

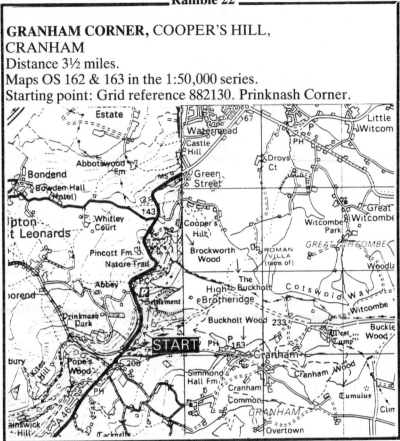

Cooper's HIll is a local Nature Reserve of 137 acres owned by the Gloucestershire County Council. It is part of an area which is Scheduled by the Nature Conservancy under the National Park and Access to the Countryside Act 1949 as a Site of Special Scientific Interest; The Gloucestershire County Council have issued a pamphlet about the area which gives guidance to Nature Trails which are marked by various coloured posts on the ground.

For this walk the simple use of a compass is essential. With the combined help of the narrative (which follows) and the Cotswold Way signs (yellow arrow and white dot) it is practicable to get to the top of Cooper's Hill without the aid of a compass. But from there, to complete the ramble through the woods, it is impossible to give satisfactory direction because of the numerous paths. Without a compass the rambler would probably begin to follow the Cotswold Way and County Council Way signs and would move round without getting to any particular objective. The rambler could use the narrative to get to the top of Cooper's Hill and then enjoy walking round and retracing his steps to the starting point but to make the complete round here described a compass is essential.

To get to the starting point: from a point about 3½ miles east of Gloucester where the A417T and A46T cross, go southwest on the A46T (i.e. towards Painswick). In about 2½ miles turn into a road on the left signposted Cranham 1 mile, Birdlip 3 miles. After about 200 yards the road forks, the one on the right being Cranham 1 mile and that on the left Birdlip 3. At this point there is a track on the left signposted Cooper's Hill 2.5 km.

......This is the start of the ramble.

Take this track to enter the wood. Follow the Cotswold Way signs (a yellow arrow and a white dot) for about 1¼ miles to the top of Coopers Hill at a flagstaff with the figure of a cock on the top. On coming to the flagstaff cease to follow the Cotswold Way signs and turn sharp right; walk in a southerly direction ascending towards a path into the wood ahead. Continue ahead in a southerly direction to a definite track. Still in the same direction follow the waymarks (a yellow arrow with a red base) for about ¾ mile to a point about 100 yards before the end of the wood. Here there is a good track to the left between two wooden posts. Descend this track to a T junction with another track: turn right and then left at another track and descend to the road at a house called Buckholt Wood.

Turn left and in a few yards take a track on the right indicated by a post with waymark (yellow arrow with red base). Follow this rather difficult narrow descending path till it comes to a junction with a wide definite track. Turn right and in a few yards at a fork bear left downhill following the waymarks. This leads to the road in Cranham.

Turn right and ascend the road for about 300 yards and enter a clearing on the right into the wood. Walk north west along ascending path with similar waymark signs for ½ mile to a road. Cross the road and go up the track opposite. In 300 yards a track is reached which is the Cotswold Way. Here turn sharp left and descend to the road, the end and the beginning of the walk.

SAPPERTON AREA

A varied pleasant walk above the River Frome.
Distance 4½ miles.
Map OS 163 in the 1:50,000 series.
Starting point: Grid reference 948033. Sapperton.

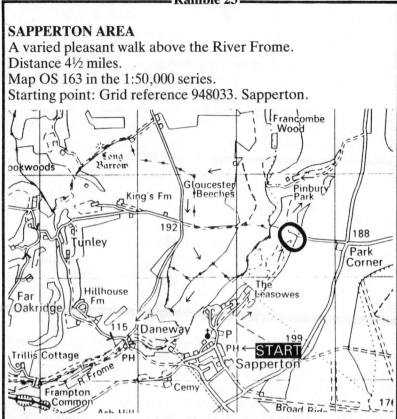

Sapperton is an interesting village. For many years it was the home of Ernest Gimson and Sydney and Ernest Barnsley who were both architects and designers of beautiful furniture. The houses they built for themselves are in the village. Ernest Gimson's genius might have been recognised if he had lived a little longer. He died in 1919 in his 55th year and was buried in Sapperton churchyard. "By Chance I did Rove" by Norman Jewson is an interesting and beautiful account of the village, the area and the period.

The book was published privately and can be borrowed from the Gloucestershire County Library.

Starting from the Bell Inn at Sapperton, go down the road, keeping the inn on the right. At the junction of roads, go through a kissing gate immediately at the beginning of the road on the right. Cross the pasture under the electricity lines to a bridle gate (i.e.

crossing it at about equal distance from the wall on each side). Continue across the next field in the same direction with a fence and hedge about 20 yards on the right. Here a gate leads into the next field, which must be crossed, with the fence still 20 yards on the right. Pass through the gate, then through some brushwood, and at the next gate enter a wood. The gate at the end of the wood leads to a piece of open pasture with trees on each side. At a fork in the track, leave the main rising track to the right, and follow the minor descending one on the left, with a distant view of the Manor House of Pinbury Park. At the bottom of the track go through a gate and continue towards Pinbury Park. Follow the bridle way round, with the wood on the right, and the valley and Pinbury Park on the left. Go ahead to a gate beyond the Park, and, having passed through, turn sharp left and walk, past a pool which is on the right, to a metalled road. Turn left and pass in front of the Park.

Pinbury Park fell into disrepair and was then taken over by Ernest Gimson and the Barnsley brothers towards the end of the 19th century. During this period they restored the house, making a charming residence, which was taken over by Lord Bathurst, on generous terms, from Gimson and the Barnsley brothers who, having married, wished to have their own houses.

Now descend along the road which becomes a track. At the bottom of the descent, cross a ford. Bear left and walk with a bank now on the left. This is covered with brushwood but there is open pasture to the right. As the track rises, it becomes enclosed with brushwood. Where this opens out, follow the definite ascending path on the right towards some derelict buildings. (Pinbury Cottage). Go through a gate, and with these buildings on the right, proceed ahead, having a wall and a fence on the right. In 500 yards at the facing wall, go through the gate, turn immediately left, and cross the first field with a wall on the left. Go over the wooden fence into the next field, and at the end of it, go over another wooden fence onto the bridle track.

The way now lies across a cultivated field in front, to a wood on the far side. Cross this field, in the same general direction as the previous one, but veer 150 yards to the left to enter a wood by a gate. Follow the track in the wood to the right. At a T junction turn right, and at another T junction bear right. On leaving the wood join a metalled road, and bear left.

Pass Daneway House which is on the left. At one period, this housed the workshop of Ernest Gimson. At the fork by the Daneway Inn, turn left, and cross the bridge. Immediately on the left, go over the stile, signposted Sapperton. Follow the green track on the raised bank, with the disused canal on the left, and a stream on the right. Cross the stile, and continue along the track between brushwood and trees, to pass a cottage on the right, and so on to an old canal tunnel. (The mason, whose duty it was to keep the tunnel in repair, lived in the cottage). The canal, which has now been filled in, ran from Framilade on the Severn to Inglesham, near Lechlade, on the Thames. The engineer for this canal tunnel was the grandson of the famous Brunel.

Go left over the top of the tunnel to a stile/fence, cross it, and then go diagonally right. The direction is towards the right of the church and a group of buildings seen ahead. At the fence, cross a stile and follow the path ahead to go over a metalled track. At the road, turn left into Sapperton.

DAGLINGWORTH, OAKLEY WOOD, OVERLEY WOOD, DUNTISBOURNE ROUSE

A very pleasant largely woodland ramble.
Distance 8½ miles.
Map OS 163 in the 1:50,000 series.
Starting point: Grid reference 993051. The village
of Daglingworth. Daglingworth is 3 miles N.N.W. of
Cirencester and lies just west of A417(T).

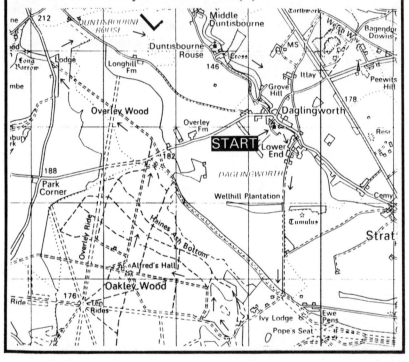

A considerable part of this ramble is not on rights of way but has been made available by the courtesy of the Earl Bathurst. Walkers and horse riders are invited to use the tracks through the woods and it is hoped that the advantages of this courtesy will be exercised with the usual responsibility which is the characteristic of nearly all ramblers.

First visit the church which is most interesting. Especially look for the Saxon stone carvings, one of which is "Christ in Majesty" and another "St. Peter with the Keys of Heaven". For further information reference can be made to an interesting booklet "Daglingworth — The Story of a Cotswold Village" by Olive M. Griffiths, which contains a chapter on Daglingworth in Roman times by J.M.C. Toynbee. It is published by the Museum Press and it is hoped that it is still in print.

Having walked up the lane from the village to the church continue ahead through a gate and follow the green lane for about 250 yards. Pass through a gate on to a road at Lower End. Follow the road round to the right. Continue straight ahead through a gate to pass between two farm buildings and then follow the green track. Continue along this well defined track for about 1¼ miles, passing a coppice on the right and then, further on, one on the left, to arrive at a facing strip of wood. Go over the cross tracks to follow a tarmacadam estate road bearing right to enter Cirencester Park. In 500 yards pass Ivy Lodge which is on the right. Continue along the road to a small triangle with some brushwood in the middle of it with a signpost "Ten Rides" and "The Wood House". At this point leave the tarmacadam road and go up a good rubble track ascending on the right i.e. towards 'Ten Rides'.

At the first cross track turn right so as to pass alongside a green ride on the left and to go deep into Oakley Wood. Immediately begin to count the tracks on the left. At the third track there is a continuation straight ahead in the form of a green track. But take this third track to the left. In ⅝ths of a mile at a cross track turn right. (It is interesting at this point to visit the nearby ruins of Alfred's Hall. It is a sham ruin built largely from the stones of Sapperton Manor House. If this is wished, then instead of turning right, continue ahead and then bear right at the distinct metalled track; but remember to continue the walk by returning to the above right turn.)

In 150 yards at a fork bear right. (The left goes to Woodhouse.) Continue for a further ½ miles ignoring all tracks to the right and left to arrive at a subsidiary road. Cross this and go down the track directly opposite leading into Overley Wood. In about 120 yards cross another track and then in about 150 yards a main junction of tracks is reached. Go over these and continue in the same direction for 100 yards to a junction of 5 tracks: take the second from the left. Do not go up the short indefinite track which leads to a wicket gate and an open field. The correct way is the first to the left of this.

Continue along the edge of the wood for nearly a mile without deviation, going past a wide green ride to a point where the wood is seen to extend to the right. Here go ahead so as to enter again deep into the wood. Bearing left continue to a five-way junction. Take the second track from the right. Pass through a gateway into an open field, and immediately turn right so as to walk with a hedge on the right. In 200 yards go over the subsidiary road and go down the track ahead. Proceed ahead along the definite track to a subsidiary road. Middle Duntisbourne is about 250 yards to the left; but turn right, and in 500 yards turn left into the main part of Duntisbourne Rouse. The church is well worth a visit, being mostly Saxon but with a Norman crypt.

Continue over the River Dunt to where the road ends at a strong left hand bend, the continuation being a green bridle track. Here go through the gate on the right signposted "Grove Hill" and "Daglingworth". Veer left uphill towards a wood. At the edge of the wood go through a gate and proceed alongside the wood which is on the right. Where the wood ends go through the gateway and continue with some cottages on the left to the metalled road; then bear right. At the T junction turn left to Daglingworth.

BREDON

A walk over Bredon with glorious views.

Distance 5¾ miles.

Map OS 150 in the 1:50,000 series.

Starting point: Grid reference 968377. Overbury Village.

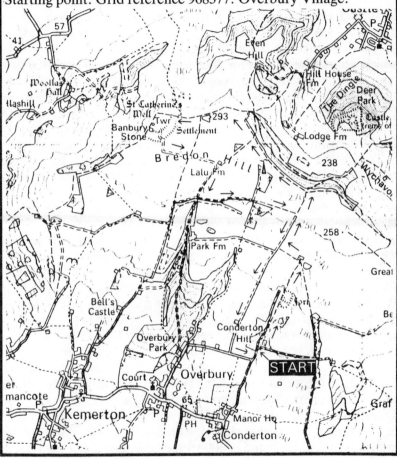

To reach Overbury from Evesham go along the Cheltenham road, A435(T), for about 7 miles and then turn off on the right through Beckford. From here Overbury is less than 2 miles away.

From Overbury, go up the road to pass to the right of the church. At the manor turn right to pass some picturesque cottages. At the T junction turn left and go up the road. Before a "No Through

Road" sign and a house named "Silver Rill", turn right. Pass a rough track on the left on the corner of which is a derelict barn, and continue to a T jucntion. Turn left.

This is the start of the ramble which can be reached by car.

In a few yards the track forks. Take the left hand one to go through the gate ahead. Follow the wire fence which is on the left to gate. Through this gate the wall on the left leads to the ruins of Shaldon Farm. Pass in front of the farm, leaving it on the right, to a gate. Follow the wall on the right to a track. **Turn right. In about 90 yards go through a gateway and then follow a line of conifers which are on the left. In another 400 yards pass through another gate** and continue straight ahead, still following a line of conifers. In another 260 yards pass through another gate, and cross a narrow field to the trees ahead. Go through the gate, and turn left along a definite track. Follow this high level track on the edge of Bredon. In a little while the radio masts will be seen away on the left.

The definite path comes to a gateway leading to a descending track. Do not go through this gateway but continue ahead with a wall to the right. The path leads to gateway. From here follow the wire fence which is up on the left. Along here there are glorious views over the Avon Valley with Pershore and many picturesque villages clearly seen. This wire fence is succeeded by a stone wall which should be followed to a gate. Pass through, and follow a stone wall which is on the right. Pass the remains of the British Encampment which are on the left and then make directly for the Bredon Tower seen on the left. At the tower turn left and walk along the embankment which leads to a cart track. **Turn right. Follow this track as it turns to the right in front of Lalu Farm.** In about 500 yards from the farm there is a gate which gives entrance into Overbury Park. Do not go through the gate but turn left along this track without deviation to a gate. Through the gate continue in the same direction on which has now become a green track to reach the T junction with another track. (This is the same track used earlier in the walk.) Turn right and descend without deviation to the minor road. Turn left and in 300 yards the beginning of the walk is reached.

The parts in bold type above are not definitive rights of way but the Overbury Estates do not object to their use by walkers on the understanding that this does not create a right of way.